THE LIFE AND TIMES OF JACQUES SAADÉ JR:

A Billionaire Businessman Of French And Lebanese Descent.

By

MERVIN S. COHEN

The entirety of the material in this publication is protected under copyright law. Reproduction, distribution, or transmission of any portion of this content in any form or manner is strictly forbidden without obtaining prior written consent from the publisher. This restriction encompasses activities such as photocopying, recording, or employing other electronic or mechanical means. Limited excerpts may be cited in critical evaluations or for specific noncommercial purposes as allowed by copyright regulations. Unauthorized use or reproduction constitutes a breach of the copyright holder's rights.

Copyright © Mervin S. Cohen, 2024.

Table of Contents

Introduction **5**

    Understanding Jacques Saadé Jr. 6

    Setting the Stage 7

Chapter 1: Early Beginnings **8**

    Growing Up in a Shipping Dynasty 9

Chapter 2: Learning the Ropes **11**

    Introduction to the Family Business 11

    Hands-On Experience in the Shipping Industry 12

Chapter 3: Taking the Helm **14**

    Succession and Leadership Transition 14

    Challenges and Opportunities 15

Chapter 4: Strategic Vision **17**

    Modernization and Expansion Efforts 17

    Pioneering Digital Solutions in Shipping 18

Chapter 5: Philanthropic Pursuits..................21

Commitment to Giving Back....................... 21

Impactful Charitable Initiatives....................22

Chapter 6: Business Ventures........................25

Leading Compagnie du Ponant................... 25

Successes and Lessons Learned.................. 26

Chapter 7: Building Global Networks...........29

Establishing International Relations............29

Strengthening CMA CGM's Position in the Industry..30

Chapter 8: Ethical Leadership.......................33

Championing Transparency and Accountability... 33

Upholding Principles of Responsibility...... 34

Chapter 9: Environmental Advocacy............37

Embracing Sustainable Shipping Practices. 37

Reducing Carbon Footprint and Promoting

Eco-Friendly Solutions.................................38

Chapter 10: Resilience and Determination.. 41

Overcoming Challenges in the Industry....... 41

Ensuring the Continuity of the Family
Legacy... 42

Chapter 11: Appreciating Art and Culture.. 44

Cultural Enrichment Beyond Business........ 44

Fostering a Diverse and Inclusive Work
Environment... 45

Chapter 12: Continuing the Legacy.............. 47

Reflections on Jacques Saadé Jr.'s Impact... 47

Looking Towards the Future........................ 49

Conclusion.. 51

Summarizing the Journey of Jacques Saadé
Jr... 51

Lessons Learned and Inspirations Gained... 53

Introduction

In the big world of ships and oceans, there's a man named Jacques Saadé Jr. He's a billionaire businessman, which means he's really, really rich. But being rich isn't the only thing that makes him special. Jacques Saadé Jr. has done many important things in his life that have helped a lot of people.

Now, let's understand who Jacques Saadé Jr. is and why he's so important. Imagine you're in a big theater, and the curtains are about to open. That's what this introduction is like – it sets the stage for the amazing story of Jacques Saadé Jr.

Understanding Jacques Saadé Jr.

Jacques Saadé Jr. is a person just like you and me, but he's also very different. He was born into a family that's famous for shipping things all over the world. Imagine you have a toy boat, and you send it to your friend who lives far away. Jacques Saadé Jr.'s family does something like that, but with really, really big boats and lots of important stuff.

Jacques Saadé Jr. learned a lot about ships and business when he was young. His family taught him how to run their shipping company. That's like if your family taught you how to ride a bike, but instead of a bike, it's a huge ship!

Setting the Stage

Now, let's imagine a big stage where a play is about to begin. That's what setting the stage means – getting ready for something exciting. Jacques Saadé Jr.'s life is like a big play, with lots of important events and adventures.

Before we dive into his story, let's think about why it's important. Jacques Saadé Jr. isn't just a rich guy. He's a leader who helps make the world a better place. His actions and decisions affect many people around the world, not just his family or friends.

Chapter 1: Early Beginnings

Jacques Saadé Jr.'s Family Background
Imagine a big tree with lots of branches. That's like Jacques Saadé Jr.'s family tree – it's really big and has been around for a long time. His family is from France and Lebanon, which are two countries far away from each other. But even though they're from different places, they all work together to run their shipping business.

Jacques Saadé Jr.'s family started their shipping company a long time ago, way back in 1978. That's even before some of your parents were born! They wanted to help people send things to different countries, so they built big ships to carry all the stuff.

Growing Up in a Shipping Dynasty

Now, let's imagine Jacques Saadé Jr. as a little boy. Instead of playing with toys like trucks or cars, he grew up around big ships and busy ports. A port is like a big playground for ships, where they come to load and unload things.

Jacques Saadé Jr. learned a lot from his family about how ships work and how to run a business. He saw how his parents and grandparents worked hard every day to make sure the ships sailed smoothly and safely.

Even though Jacques Saadé Jr. was just a kid, he was already learning important things that would help him later in life. He learned about teamwork and responsibility, just like when you work together with your friends to build a sandcastle at the beach.

Chapter 2: Learning the Ropes

Introduction to the Family Business

Imagine walking into a big, bustling warehouse filled with crates and containers. That's what it was like for Jacques Saadé Jr. when he first stepped into the world of his family's shipping business. From a young age, he was eager to learn and eager to help.

His family taught him everything about the business – from how to load a ship with cargo to how to make sure it got to its destination on time. Jacques Saadé Jr. listened carefully and asked lots of questions. He wanted to understand every part of the process, from start to finish.

Hands-On Experience in the Shipping Industry

But Jacques Saadé Jr. didn't just learn by listening – he learned by doing. He rolled up his sleeves and got his hands dirty, working alongside the crew on the ships and in the ports. He helped load and unload cargo, tie down the ropes, and navigate the waters.

It wasn't always easy – sometimes the seas were rough, and the work was hard. But Jacques Saadé Jr. didn't mind. He loved being out on the water, feeling the wind in his hair and the spray of the sea on his face.

And as he worked, he learned valuable lessons about teamwork, leadership, and perseverance. He saw how important it was for everyone to work together to make sure the job got done right. And he learned that even when things got tough, it was important to keep going and never give up.

Chapter 3: Taking the Helm

Succession and Leadership Transition

When Jacques Saadé Sr., Jacques Saadé Jr.'s father, passed away, it was time for Jacques Saadé Jr. to take charge. Imagine passing a baton in a relay race – that's what succession is like. Jacques Saadé Jr. was ready to carry on his father's legacy and lead the family business into the future.

But becoming the leader wasn't just about sitting in a big chair and giving orders. Jacques Saadé Jr. had to earn the trust and respect of the people who worked for the company. He had to show them that he was capable and committed to carrying on the family's mission.

Challenges and Opportunities

Leading a big shipping company isn't always smooth sailing – there are bound to be storms along the way. Jacques Saadé Jr. faced many challenges as he took the helm of the family business. Imagine trying to navigate through rough seas with big waves crashing all around you – that's what it was like for Jacques Saadé Jr.

But with every challenge, there's also an opportunity. Jacques Saadé Jr. saw potential where others saw obstacles. He embraced new technologies and innovations to make the company stronger and more efficient. He looked for ways to expand into new markets and reach more customers around the world.

And through it all, Jacques Saadé Jr. never lost sight of his father's vision. He knew that the company's success wasn't just about making money – it was about making a positive impact on the world. So he worked tirelessly to uphold the values of integrity, responsibility, and excellence that his father had instilled in him.

Chapter 4: Strategic Vision

Modernization and Expansion Efforts

Jacques Saadé Jr. had big dreams for the family business. He wanted to take it to new heights and reach even more people around the world. But to do that, he knew he needed to modernize and expand.

Imagine a house that's been around for a long time – it might need some renovations and additions to keep it strong and sturdy. That's what Jacques Saadé Jr. did with the family business. He invested in new ships and equipment to make sure they could keep up with the demands of the modern world.

But modernization wasn't just about shiny new ships – it was also about finding new ways to do things better and faster. Jacques Saadé Jr. introduced new technologies and systems to streamline operations and improve efficiency. He looked for ways to reduce waste and minimize environmental impact, showing that success doesn't have to come at the expense of the planet.

Pioneering Digital Solutions in Shipping

One of Jacques Saadé Jr.'s biggest achievements was pioneering digital solutions in the shipping industry. Imagine a world where you can track a package from the moment it leaves the warehouse to the moment it arrives at your doorstep – that's the world Jacques Saadé Jr. helped create.

He saw the potential of digital technology to revolutionize the way goods were shipped around the world. He invested in state-of-the-art tracking systems and communication networks to make sure that every shipment was monitored and managed with precision.

But Jacques Saadé Jr. didn't stop there – he also saw the potential of digital technology to connect people and businesses in new and exciting ways. He invested in online platforms and marketplaces to make it easier for customers to buy and sell goods across borders, opening up new opportunities for trade and commerce.

Chapter 5: Philanthropic Pursuits

Commitment to Giving Back

Jacques Saadé Jr. believes in the importance of helping others and giving back to the community. Just like sharing your toys with your friends, Jacques Saadé Jr. shares his wealth and resources to make the world a better place.

He understands that not everyone is as fortunate as he is, so he makes it a priority to lend a helping hand to those in need. Whether it's providing food and shelter to the homeless, or supporting education and healthcare programs, Jacques Saadé Jr. is always there to offer support.

But giving back isn't just about writing a big check – it's about making a real difference in people's lives. Jacques Saadé Jr. gets personally involved in charitable activities, volunteering his time and expertise to help those who need it most.

Impactful Charitable Initiatives

Jacques Saadé Jr. doesn't just talk the talk – he walks the walk. He has spearheaded many charitable initiatives that have had a positive impact on communities around the world.

For example, he has supported initiatives to provide clean water and sanitation to people in developing countries. He knows that clean water is essential for good health and sanitation, so he works to ensure that everyone has access to this basic necessity.

Jacques Saadé Jr. has also been a champion for education, believing that every child deserves the opportunity to learn and grow. He has supported schools and educational programs in underserved communities, giving children the tools they need to build a brighter future.

And when disaster strikes, Jacques Saadé Jr. is quick to lend a helping hand. Whether it's providing emergency relief to victims of natural disasters or supporting rebuilding efforts in affected communities, he is always there to offer support and assistance.

Chapter 6: Business Ventures

Leading Compagnie du Ponant

Jacques Saadé Jr. didn't just stick to the family business – he also ventured into other exciting opportunities. One of his biggest ventures was leading Compagnie du Ponant, a luxury cruise company.

Imagine sailing on a big ship with fancy rooms and delicious food – that's what Compagnie du Ponant offered to its guests. Jacques Saadé Jr. was at the helm, steering the company towards success.

Under his leadership, Compagnie du Ponant saw many exciting developments. Jacques

Saadé Jr. brought his expertise in the shipping industry to the world of luxury cruises, ensuring that guests had an unforgettable experience on board.

Successes and Lessons Learned

Running a luxury cruise company wasn't always smooth sailing. Jacques Saadé Jr. faced many challenges along the way, but he didn't let them stop him. Instead, he used them as opportunities to learn and grow.

One of the biggest lessons Jacques Saadé Jr. learned was the importance of listening to his customers. Just like how you listen to your friends when they talk to you, Jacques Saadé Jr. listened to what his guests wanted and made sure to provide it.

He also learned the importance of teamwork and collaboration. Running a big company like Compagnie du Ponant wasn't something Jacques Saadé Jr. could do alone – he needed the help of his dedicated team. Together, they worked hard to make sure that every guest had a fantastic experience.

And in the end, all of Jacques Saadé Jr.'s hard work paid off. Compagnie du Ponant became known as one of the top luxury cruise companies in the world, thanks to his leadership and vision.

But Jacques Saadé Jr. didn't just focus on the successes – he also learned from the failures. He understood that not every idea would work out, but that didn't mean he should give up. Instead, he used every experience as an opportunity to grow and improve.

Chapter 7: Building Global Networks

Establishing International Relations

Just like making friends in school, Jacques Saadé Jr. knew the importance of building good relationships with people from all over the world. He understood that having friends in different countries could help his family's shipping business grow and succeed.

So, Jacques Saadé Jr. traveled far and wide, meeting with business leaders and government officials in countries around the world. He listened to their ideas and shared his own, working together to find ways to make shipping easier and more efficient.

But building international relations wasn't just about shaking hands and smiling for the cameras – it was about building trust and understanding. Jacques Saadé Jr. took the time to learn about different cultures and customs, respecting the differences while finding common ground.

Strengthening CMA CGM's Position in the Industry

As Jacques Saadé Jr. built relationships around the world, he also worked hard to strengthen CMA CGM's position in the shipping industry. Imagine playing a game of tug-of-war – Jacques Saadé Jr. wanted to make sure that CMA CGM was always on the winning side.

He invested in new ships and technology to make sure that CMA CGM could compete with the biggest players in the industry. He also expanded the company's reach, opening new offices and ports in strategic locations around the world.

But it wasn't just about being the biggest – it was also about being the best. Jacques Saadé Jr. focused on providing top-notch service to his customers, making sure that their goods were delivered safely and on time.

And as CMA CGM's reputation grew, so did its influence in the industry. Other companies looked to CMA CGM as a leader, following its example and learning from its success.

Chapter 8: Ethical Leadership

Championing Transparency and Accountability

Jacques Saadé Jr. believed in being open and honest in all his dealings. Just like how you tell the truth to your friends and family, Jacques Saadé Jr. made sure that CMA CGM was transparent about its actions and decisions.

He believed that transparency builds trust. Imagine playing a game of hide and seek – if you can't see the other players, it's hard to trust them. Jacques Saadé Jr. wanted CMA CGM to be like an open book, where everyone could see what was happening and trust that everything was being done the right way.

But transparency wasn't just about showing off – it was also about taking responsibility. Jacques Saadé Jr. made sure that CMA CGM took responsibility for its actions, whether they were good or bad. Just like how you take responsibility for your actions, Jacques Saadé Jr. wanted CMA CGM to own up to its mistakes and learn from them.

Upholding Principles of Responsibility

Jacques Saadé Jr. believed that with great power comes great responsibility. Just like how you take care of your toys and pets,

Jacques Saadé Jr. made sure that CMA CGM took care of its employees, customers, and the environment.

He understood that CMA CGM had a big impact on the world – from the people who worked for the company to the communities it served. So he made it a priority to do things the right way, even if it meant taking the harder path.

For example, Jacques Saadé Jr. was committed to protecting the environment. He knew that shipping could have a big impact on the planet, so he invested in eco-friendly technologies and practices to minimize CMA CGM's carbon footprint.

He also believed in treating people with respect and dignity. Just like how you treat your friends and family with kindness, Jacques Saadé Jr. made sure that CMA CGM treated its employees and customers with fairness and respect.

Chapter 9: Environmental Advocacy

Embracing Sustainable Shipping Practices

Jacques Saadé Jr. believed in taking care of the planet, just like how you take care of your toys and pets. He understood that shipping could have a big impact on the environment, so he made it his mission to find ways to do it in a more sustainable way.

One way Jacques Saadé Jr. did this was by investing in eco-friendly technologies. Imagine a car that runs on clean energy – Jacques Saadé Jr. wanted CMA CGM's ships to be like that, running on cleaner fuels and emitting fewer harmful gases.

He also looked for ways to reduce waste and pollution. Just like how you recycle your paper and plastic, Jacques Saadé Jr. implemented practices to minimize CMA CGM's impact on the oceans and marine life.

Reducing Carbon Footprint and Promoting Eco-Friendly Solutions

One of Jacques Saadé Jr.'s biggest achievements was reducing CMA CGM's carbon footprint. Imagine a giant footprint in the sand – that's how much carbon dioxide CMA CGM's ships used to emit. But thanks to Jacques Saadé Jr.'s efforts, that footprint got smaller and smaller over time.

He did this by investing in new technologies and practices that were kinder to the planet. For example, he looked for ways to make CMA CGM's ships more fuel-efficient, so they used less fuel and emitted fewer greenhouse gases.

He also promoted eco-friendly solutions throughout the company. Just like how you tell your friends about your favorite toys, Jacques Saadé Jr. encouraged CMA CGM's employees to find new ways to be more sustainable in their work.

And it wasn't just about what happened on the ships – Jacques Saadé Jr. also looked at the bigger picture. He supported initiatives to protect marine habitats and wildlife, knowing that healthy oceans are essential for a healthy planet.

Chapter 10: Resilience and Determination

Overcoming Challenges in the Industry

Running a big shipping company like CMA CGM wasn't always smooth sailing for Jacques Saadé Jr. He faced many challenges along the way, just like how you might face obstacles when building a big tower with blocks.

One of the biggest challenges Jacques Saadé Jr. faced was competition. Imagine playing a game of soccer against a team that's bigger and stronger than yours – that's what it was like for CMA CGM. But instead of giving up,

Jacques Saadé Jr. and his team worked harder and smarter to stay ahead.

He also faced challenges from things like economic downturns and changes in the industry. Imagine trying to build a sandcastle at the beach, but the waves keep washing it away – that's what it was like for Jacques Saadé Jr. But instead of getting discouraged, he kept rebuilding and adapting to the changing tides.

Ensuring the Continuity of the Family Legacy

But through it all, Jacques Saadé Jr. remained determined to ensure the continuity of the family legacy. Just like how you pass on your favorite toys to your little brother or sister, Jacques Saadé Jr. wanted to pass on the family business to future generations.

He knew that the family legacy wasn't just about making money – it was about making a positive impact on the world. So he worked tirelessly to make sure that CMA CGM continued to grow and succeed, just like his father had wanted.

Jacques Saadé Jr. also understood the importance of staying true to the family's values and principles. Just like how you follow the rules when playing a game, Jacques Saadé Jr. made sure that CMA CGM operated with integrity and responsibility.

Chapter 11: Appreciating Art and Culture

Cultural Enrichment Beyond Business

Jacques Saadé Jr. believed in the importance of appreciating art and culture, just like how you enjoy playing with different toys and colors. He understood that there's more to life than just work – there's beauty and creativity all around us.

So, Jacques Saadé Jr. made time to explore art and culture in all its forms. He visited museums and galleries, attended concerts and performances, and traveled to new places to experience different cultures. Just like how you go on adventures to discover new things, Jacques Saadé Jr. embarked on cultural journeys to enrich his life.

But his appreciation for art and culture didn't stop there – he also brought it into his work. Just like how you decorate your room with your favorite things, Jacques Saadé Jr. infused art and culture into the work environment at CMA CGM, creating a space that was inspiring and vibrant.

Fostering a Diverse and Inclusive Work Environment

Jacques Saadé Jr. believed in the power of diversity and inclusion, just like how you enjoy playing with friends from different backgrounds. He understood that when people from different cultures and perspectives come together, amazing things can happen.

So, Jacques Saadé Jr. worked hard to foster a diverse and inclusive work environment at CMA CGM. He hired people from all over the world, regardless of their race, gender, or background. Just like how you include everyone when playing a game, Jacques Saadé Jr. made sure that everyone at CMA CGM felt valued and respected.

He also encouraged open dialogue and collaboration, just like how you share ideas with your friends. Jacques Saadé Jr. wanted everyone at CMA CGM to feel comfortable expressing themselves and contributing their unique perspectives to the team.

Chapter 12: Continuing the Legacy

Reflections on Jacques Saadé Jr.'s Impact

Jacques Saadé Jr. made a big impact on the world, just like how a big rock creates ripples in a pond. He dedicated his life to building and growing CMA CGM, but his influence extended far beyond the shipping industry.

One of Jacques Saadé Jr.'s biggest contributions was his commitment to ethical leadership. He showed that businesses can be successful while still being kind to the planet and treating people with respect. Just like how you share your toys with your friends, Jacques Saadé Jr. believed in sharing his success with others and making the world a better place.

He also believed in the power of diversity and inclusion. Just like how you enjoy playing with friends from different backgrounds, Jacques Saadé Jr. understood that when people from different cultures and perspectives come together, amazing things can happen. He created a work environment at CMA CGM where everyone felt valued and respected, regardless of their race, gender, or background.

But perhaps Jacques Saadé Jr.'s greatest legacy was his determination to ensure the continuity of the family legacy. Just like how you pass on your favorite toys to your little brother or sister, Jacques Saadé Jr. wanted to pass on the family business to future generations. He worked tirelessly to make sure that CMA CGM continued to grow and succeed, just like his father had wanted.

Looking Towards the Future

As we look towards the future, Jacques Saadé Jr.'s legacy continues to inspire and guide us. His commitment to ethical leadership, environmental advocacy, and diversity and inclusion will continue to shape the way businesses operate for years to come.

But the future is also full of new challenges and opportunities. Just like how you learn new things every day, we must continue to adapt and innovate to stay ahead in a rapidly changing world. But as long as we stay true to the values and principles that Jacques Saadé Jr. taught us, we can overcome any obstacle that comes our way.

Conclusion

Summarizing the Journey of Jacques Saadé Jr.

Jacques Saadé Jr. was a remarkable individual who made a profound impact on the world. He was born into a family legacy of shipping magnates and took the helm of CMA CGM, transforming it into one of the largest and most successful shipping companies in the world.

From an early age, Jacques Saadé Jr. was immersed in the family business, learning the ropes and gaining hands-on experience in the shipping industry. He showed resilience and determination in overcoming challenges, steering CMA CGM through rough seas and ensuring its continuous growth and success.

Jacques Saadé Jr. was not just a businessman – he was a visionary leader who championed ethical business practices, environmental stewardship, and diversity and inclusion. He believed in transparency, accountability, and responsibility, setting a shining example for others to follow.

His commitment to giving back to society and fostering a diverse and inclusive work environment demonstrated his deep sense of humanity and compassion. Jacques Saadé Jr. left behind a legacy of integrity, innovation, and excellence that continues to inspire and guide us today.

Lessons Learned and Inspirations Gained

Through Jacques Saadé Jr.'s journey, we have learned valuable lessons that can guide us in both our personal and professional lives.

Firstly, Jacques Saadé Jr. taught us the importance of perseverance and resilience in the face of adversity. No matter how tough the challenges may seem, with determination and perseverance, we can overcome them and emerge stronger than before.

Secondly, Jacques Saadé Jr. showed us the power of ethical leadership and responsible business practices. By prioritizing transparency, accountability, and environmental stewardship, we can create a better and more sustainable future for all.

Additionally, Jacques Saadé Jr. emphasized the significance of diversity and inclusion in driving innovation and success. When we embrace diversity and foster an inclusive work environment, we unlock the full potential of our teams and organizations.

Finally, Jacques Saadé Jr. inspired us to dream big and think outside the box. He showed us that with vision, passion, and hard work, anything is possible, and we can achieve greatness beyond our wildest imagination.

www.ingramcontent.com/pod-product-compliance
Lightning Source LLC
Chambersburg PA
CBHW050244230526
45470CB00005B/2103